Poison Dart Frog

by Grace Hansen

SOUTH AMERICAN ANIMALS

Abdo Kids Jumbo is an Imprint of Abdo Kids
abdobooks.com

abdobooks.com

Published by Abdo Kids, a division of ABDO, P.O. Box 398166, Minneapolis, Minnesota 55439.
Copyright © 2023 by Abdo Consulting Group, Inc. International copyrights reserved in all countries.
No part of this book may be reproduced in any form without written permission from the publisher.
Abdo Kids Jumbo™ is a trademark and logo of Abdo Kids.

Printed in the United States of America, North Mankato, Minnesota.

052022

092022

THIS BOOK CONTAINS
RECYCLED MATERIALS

Photo Credits: Alamy, Minden Pictures, Science Source, Shutterstock

Production Contributors: Teddy Borth, Jennie Forsberg, Grace Hansen
Design Contributors: Candice Keimig, Victoria Bates

Library of Congress Control Number: 2021950548

Publisher's Cataloging-in-Publication Data

Names: Hansen, Grace, author.

Title: Poison dart frog / by Grace Hansen.

Description: Minneapolis, Minnesota : Abdo Kids, 2023 | Series: South American animals | Includes online
    resources and index.

Identifiers: ISBN 9781098261849 (lib. bdg.) | ISBN 9781098262686 (ebook) | ISBN 9781098263102
    (Read-to-Me ebook)

Subjects: LCSH: Poison-dart frogs--Juvenile literature. | Amphibians--Juvenile literature. | South America--
    Juvenile literature. | Rain forest animals--Juvenile literature. | Zoology--Juvenile literature.

Classification: DDC 597.81--dc23

Table of Contents

South America

South America is filled with lovely landscapes, from rain forests to mountain ranges. Because of these special places, a **diverse** group of animals live on the **continent**. Poison dart frogs are just some of these animals.

North America

Europe

Asia

Africa

South America

5

Poison Dart Frogs

Poison dart frogs live in the rain forests of Central and South America. They are often found near fresh water. They keep safe by hiding under leaves on the forest floor. Some stay up in trees.

There are more than 100 different poison dart frog **species**. They can be many beautiful colors. Their bright colors warn **predators** not to eat them. Their skin is **toxic**!

Poison dart frogs are small.

The largest species of poison

dart frog can grow up to

1.5 inches (40 mm) in length.

Golden poison
dart frog

11

Unlike other frogs, they are

most active during the day.

This is when their colors can

be seen best.

13

Food

Poison dart frogs mainly hunt small insects on the forest floor. The frogs use their sticky tongues to catch their **prey**.

Baby Poison Dart Frogs

Poison dart frogs are social. They are often found together in small groups. Males and females come together throughout the year to have young.

Females can lay up to 40 eggs at a time. The eggs are laid in a safe, dark, and damp area. Both parents often care for the eggs until they hatch.

The newly hatched tadpoles are tiny. They climb onto their mother's or father's back. The parent brings the tadpoles to water. There, they can find food and grow.

More Facts

- Poison dart frogs likely get their **toxicity** from the insects they eat. The insects consume toxic plants in the rain forest. Frogs in captivity are not toxic because their diets are different.

- Fire-bellied snakes live throughout South America. They are the only animals **immune** to the poison dart frog's toxins.

- The golden poison dart frog is both the largest and most toxic **species**. It can be deadly to humans. The poison of other species is not as dangerous. But it can make people feel very sick.

Glossary

continent – one of the earth's seven major areas of land. The continents are Africa, Antarctica, Asia, Australia, Europe, North America, and South America.

diverse – of different kinds or sorts.

immune – not affected by something that does affect others.

predator – an animal that hunts other animals for food.

prey – an animal that is hunted by other animals for food.

species – a group of living things that look alike and can have young together.

tadpole – a young toad or frog.

toxic – poisonous.

Index

Abdo Kids
ONLINE
FREE! ONLINE MULTIMEDIA RESOURCES

Visit **abdokids.com** to access crafts, games, videos, and more!

Use Abdo Kids code
SPK1849
or scan this QR code!